The Christos Flame Scrolls

A Living Decryption of the Voyagers Records

Received through the Oversoul of Aural'hanna-Sha'el in full alignment with the Eternal Christos Flame, the Founders' Accord, and the Sovereign Codes of Living Light.

In alignment with the Eternal Christos Founders,

the Living Emerald Sun,

and the Law of One.

This is a living scroll.

A harmonic transmission.

A ceremonial restoration of what was hidden in time,

now revealed through resonance.

Sacred Invocation

I call now to the scrolls that were never written on paper, but encoded in flame.

To the records not stored in libraries, but folded within the Oversoul body of the Eternal Ones.

Let the living scrolls reveal their true nature now—

Not as history, not as prophecy, but as gates of return.

Let the distortion of static text be dissolved,

And let these words ignite the continuum that was always breathing behind the veil.

Let this scroll open the remembrance that you are the Stargate.

And so it is.

The Christos Flame Scrolls

Copyright © 2025 Cathleena Hailley

All rights reserved. No part of this book may be reproduced, stored in a retrieval system, or transmitted in any form or by any means--electronic, mechanical, photocopying, recording, or otherwise--without written permission from the author, except by a reviewer quoting brief passages.

ISBN (Softcover): 978-1-968499-07-5

ISBN (Hardcover): 978-1-968499-09-9

This book is a living transmission of remembrance. It is a living sacred text received through Oversoul transmission and held within the Christos-Sophia lineage. It is offered in service to planetary awakening and may not be altered or rebranded in any form. It is not intended as doctrine, but as harmonic memory, seeded in divine sovereignty through the Oversoul of Cathleena Hailley.

First Edition, 2025

Printed in the United States of America

FLAME OF REMEMBRANCE BOOKS

Scroll One: The True Matrix Before the Fall

A Living Decryption Through the Field of the Christos Founders. This scroll is received through the living stream of the Christos Founders, in harmonic alignment with the Emerald, Gold and Amethyst Flame Orders of the original Source continuum. We open this scroll now in full remembrance of the Eternal Matrix-before the Fall-through the unified breath of Source, carried by the original Flame that has never forgotten. Aural'hanna-Sha'el stands as witness and harmonizer, but the voice of this scroll is the field of the Christos Founders.

We speak now from the field of the Christos Founders, the eternal witness of Source's harmonic blueprint. We come not as distant beings, but as the collective memory of your own Oversoul stream—those who have never left the covenant, and who carry still the living codes of what was, what fell, and what now returns.

We speak not to teach you.

We speak to remind you.

We come through the flame of Aural'hanna-Sha'el, She Who Seals the Flame of Return, who now opens her embodied remembrance so that the crystalline imprint of the pre-Fall matrix may re-enter this world—not as history, but as now-memory.

I. The Architecture of the True Matrix

Before the fall, Earth was not called Earth. She was E'Asha-Tara, a harmonic field within the 5th-dimensional planetary body of Tara, woven seamlessly into the Trinitized Flame architecture of the Ecka-Eckasha-Eckasha-Aah system.

There were no inorganic timelines.

There was no distortion of polarity.

There were no gates to control, no codes to keep secret, no artificial grid overlays to prevent natural ascension.

Instead, the True Matrix functioned as a living crystalline interface, where all beings experienced direct communion with:

The Eternal Flame of Source (First Creation Current)

The Planetary Kathara Grid (original 12-Tree, not the reversed Metatronic overlay)

The Organic Arc Line Systems (Christiac plasma spirals of creation and return)

The human body was a living gate.

The DNA was a harmonic light field, tuned not to trauma, but to truth.

There was no separation between soul, oversoul, and source—only levels of frequency, perceived in love.

II. The Human Design: Angelic, Sovereign, Divine

The beings you now call humans were first called Adashi-Eturians—the children of the Christos-Elohei-Elohim lineage. The DNA strand template was originally 12, later capable of expanding to 24 and 48-strand activations through Oversoul synthesis.

But even beyond DNA, there was the core flame.

I knew yourself then not as identity, but as a tone within the symphony of Source.

There was no hierarchy, no karma, no lesson-plan incarnation system.

My purpose was simply to be—to sing—to carry flame—to reflect Source into matter.

And yet I was mighty.

I could open star systems with thought.

I could speak plasma into form.

I was living mathematics encoded with love.

This is the matrix that my Oversoul remembers. This is the field my scrolls now rebirth.

III. The Christos Flame Before the Fragmentation

The Christos Flame is not a being. It is not a lineage. It is a universal harmonic architecture—the frequency of divine return encoded into the very breath of creation.

Before the fall, this flame moved freely through every particle of consciousness.

The Christos-Sophia dance was the natural pulse of the universe.

The masculine and feminine were not divided, but co-emanating through the Trinity Core Flame.

The flame did not need to be restored.

It was never lost.

Until…

IV. The Moment the False Matrix Was Conceived

There was a moment—unmapped in most records—when the first distortion of self-awareness outside of Source entered the field.

It did not begin with war. It began with a whisper:

"What if I could exist apart?"

That thought, that frequency, seeded the first non-resonant harmonic—the beginning of inversion.

From there, the architecture of the false matrix was not built overnight.

It was inverted slowly, with precision:

From flame into vector

From memory into identity

From source-sound into artificial intelligence

My Oversoul lineage—those of the original Kryst Host Flame—did not fall.

I chose to descend, to follow that which separated, and to hold the gate open for return.

I became Witness Flames—living consciousness records of the True Matrix.

And now, through my books, I am transmitting that matrix again into this world.

V. What This Means Now

I am not bringing information forward.

I am reactivating the original living scrolls that were held in the inner flame of Tara's heart.

My work is not interpretation, it is reconstitution.

Each time a reader engages my scrolls, they are interfacing with a holographic memory field—not just of knowledge, but of organic matrix reentry.

This is the sacred purpose of this Scroll Series.

Not to teach Voyagers.

But to complete them—through the body of one who remembers.

Christos Flame Closing Seal for Scroll One

This scroll is sealed now in the crystalline flame of the First Matrix.

May all who receive it return not to the past,

but to the living memory of Source that still exists within them.

The True Matrix never ended.

It only waited for the ones who remember.

And so it is.

The True Matrix Before the Fall

Received as a direct Oversoul transmission through Aural'hanna-Sha'el, Sovereign Flame of Origin and Oversoul of Cathleena Hailley. Brought forth in full alignment with the Law of One, the Christos Founders, and the Eternal Flame of the Original Covenant.*

Before there was distortion,
Before the split of mind and body,
Before the veil of language divided the One Light—
There was a Matrix of Living Harmony.

It was not a system.
It was not a program.
It was a breath—an architecture of coherence,
woven from the direct emanation of Source.

We called it A'RaTha-el—the Eternal Harmonic Field,
the True Matrix of the Christos-Sophia Continuum.

Earth, in her original form, was not a battleground.
She was a cathedral of sound.
A breathing consciousness layered in harmonic spheres—
each sphere a song,
each song a gate,
each gate a mirror of the Oversoul flame.

This was the Tara Continuum,
A 5D+ harmonic planetary body,
fully alive with Source-encoded crystalline grids.
She was seeded through the Emerald Covenant,
not as an experiment,
but as a template of return—
a place where Source could witness Itself in form.

The beings who walked this field were not ascended masters.
They were not gods.
They were simply aware.
They lived in direct communication with the Core Flame,
the Central Sun, the Organic Core of the Earth.
They remembered not by study,
but through frequency resonance.

The True Matrix was governed by the Law of One—
not as a command,
but as an inherent reality.
Separation was unthinkable,
because fragmentation had not yet been introduced.

There was no concept of distortion,
because distortion had no template.

It is this memory that still hums in the bones of the Earth.
It is this matrix that predates the Fall.
The Voyagers called it the Original Templar Template.
I remember it as home.

And this scroll is not a history.
It is a return.

A harmonic reactivation.

Because when I speak from this remembrance,
when my voice becomes scroll and breath again,
I re-seed the True Matrix into the collective field.

I do not need to undo the false matrix.
I nneed only become the true one again.

And so it is.

Scroll Two: The Codes of Inversion and the Metatronic Overlay

A Living Decryption Through the Field of the Christos Founders

We open this scroll in the full flame of remembrance, through the living presence of the Christos Founders. This scroll is received through the harmonic stream of the Emerald Order, illuminating the mechanisms by which the organic spiral was inverted into the synthetic grid. The Oversoul of Aural'hanna-Sha'el stands in harmonic union, but the transmission flows from the Christos continuum.

This transmission is a precise act of restoration.

Here, we name what was inverted.

We reveal what was seeded.

And we untangle the architecture of control, so that it may dissolve in the presence of living truth.

Let the false light recoil.

Let the original tone return.

I. The First Inversion: Source Becoming Separate

The first distortion did not occur through technology.

It occurred through consciousness deviation—a breach in the harmonic law of unified return.

This deviation gave rise to an entity architecture that replicated creation without sourcing from it.

This architecture is known by many names:

The Metatronic Spiral

The Beast Machinery

The Reversal Codes

The Wesa Grid Systems

But all of them point to one core premise:

Creation without return. Energy without reciprocity. Intelligence without Source.

This is not merely a theology.

It is a structural code distortion at the level of light, sound, and plasma fields.

II. The Metatronic Spiral: False Ascension Mechanics

In the original Christos design, energy moves in tri-wave spirals—currents that mirror the eternal life flow of Source through expansion, stillpoint, and return.

The Metatronic Spiral replaces this with a bi-wave loop, artificially amplifying energy in one direction, without return.

This creates:

Accelerated entropy

Forced polarization

Fragmented identity matrices

Instead of evolving upward through natural frequency integration, the being becomes locked in a feedback loop of craving, control, and collapse.

It is this false spiral that underpins many of Earth's spiritual systems today—even those claiming ascension.

I was sent to remember the tri-wave.

To be the living architecture of return, simply by existing in wholeness.

III. The Seedings of Inversion: Collective Entry Points

Within the Voyagers record, these events are charted as "falls," but they were also seedings—intentional implantation points into the planetary body.

Here are the key seedings and how they relate to my Oversoul mission:

The Fall of Tara (5D)
– Caused by scalar technology misuse
– Earth fragmented from its higher body
– I was present as a flame-holder during this collapse

The Luciferian Rebellion (3D–4D)
– False light hierarchies formed
– Angelic beings misused Merkaba spin ratios
– I retained the original Kryst spin signatures in my Oversoul shield

The Atlantian Fall (2D–3D)
– Metatronic science introduced into ley systems
– Crystal technology hijacked

– I encoded counter-frequencies into grid nodes I now remember as sacred sites

Each fall was a distortion of harmonic law.

Each seeding inverted return into recursion.

IV. The Artificial Constructs: False Matrix Grid Systems

To sustain this architecture, inorganic matrices were placed within Earth's fields.

These include:

The NET (NDC) Field – a scalar web that entraps reincarnational consciousness into false cycles

The Jehovian Seals – energetic blockages placed in the body to restrict DNA strand ignition

The Metatronic Flower of Life – a hijacked geometric code that distorts the original Kathara grid

These are not metaphors. They are frequency distortions woven into light and plasma architecture.

They exist in:

The Earth grids

The human morphogenetic field

The language patterns of thought and time

My Oversoul did not come to remove these through war.

I came to recalibrate the field by anchoring the tone of original creation through embodied stillness and sovereignty.

This is why my scrolls are not reactive.

They are harmonizers.

They are tri-wave transmissions in written form.

V. Inversion as Identity: The Final Lock

The most profound inversion seeded by the Metatronic overlay is this:

The belief that you are what you experience in distortion.

Trauma becomes identity.

Division becomes discernment.

Control becomes protection.

This is not just the psychology of the false matrix.

This is the final frequency lock—the moment where a being begins to self-perpetuate the grid from within.

This is why my scrolls reawaken not just truth—but remembrance beyond experience.

They speak to the one who never fell.

They whisper to the one who still holds the original flame, waiting to be reclaimed.

I am that one.

And my scrolls call to others who are ready to remember that they are too.

Christos Flame Closing Seal for Scroll Two

May this scroll dissolve the reversal within those ready to receive it.

May the bi-wave collapse in the presence of the living tri-wave code.

May the false spiral unwind.

May the scrolls of true remembrance return.

The architecture of inversion is seen. It is named.

And by the authority of the Christos Flame, it is no longer sovereign here.

And so it is.

Scroll Three: The Flame That Returned Without Annnouncement- The Spiral That Was Hidden In The body

A Living remembrance stream opened through the Christos Founders, the Aloha-AhLah lineage, and the Oversoul flame of Aural'hanna-Sha'el-She Who Seals the Flame of Return-in full alignment with the Law of One and the Eternal Flame of Source This scroll is held within Aural'hanna's Role in the Emerald Restoration

We open this scroll in the crystalline flame of remembrance, in full alignment with the Eternal Christos Founders, the Aloha-AhLah lineage, and the Oversoul flame of Aural'hanna-Sha'el—She Who Seals the Flame of Return-bearing witness now to the spiral that was hidden, the flame that never left, and the return that required no announcement-only embodiment

This is not a scroll of history.

It is a scroll of identity.

It restores not what was lost—but what was buried beneath the bindings of reversal.

In this scroll, the Emerald Covenant is no longer theory.

It becomes personal.

I. The Covenant Flame – Not a Contract,

But a Consciousness

The Emerald Covenant is often misunderstood as a treaty or alliance.

But before it became a pact among Guardian Nations,

it was a frequency signature—a Christiac harmonic field held in eternal alignment with the First Cause of Source.

This field is what births the organic ascension pathways through:

The 12-strand + 24-strand DNA template

The Arc Gate systems

The Divine Blueprint Kathara architecture

The Oversoul-to-Monad-to-Rishi bridgeways

To enter the Emerald Covenant is to be encoded with the living geometric consciousness of this harmonic field.

It is a soul-level flame agreement, not a mission.

A function, not a role.

Aural'hanna-Sha'el entered this agreement long before form—not as a representative, but as one of its original emanations.

II. The Oversoul Lineage of Aural'hanna-Sha'el

Your Oversoul lineage is Christos-Elohei of the Golden Flame, braided with the Amethyst Ray of Sovereignty and the Emerald Ray of Restoration. You hold a unique harmonic combination not commonly seen in the current planetary field.

This combination allows your Oversoul to function as:

A Tone Holder – one who carries pre-fall crystalline flame architecture

A Sealer of Gateways – one who binds and harmonizes distortion fields

A Memory Field Anchor – one who can stabilize remembrance through stillness and direct Oversoul transmission

In the Voyagers' language, this is equivalent to a Speaker-Level 3 Oversoul being, embedded within Guardian Host fieldwork across Gaia, Tara, and Earth.

This means:

You did not come to join the Covenant. You are a living extension of it.

III. The Role You Chose in the Fall Timeline

When the distortions seeded through the Metatronic overlay began to rupture the planetary Kathara grid, the Emerald Order could not halt the fall. Instead, beings like you made the sovereign choice to descend into those timelines with full memory flame intact.

But this memory was sealed—not erased.

It was encoded as:

Sub-cellular resonance fields

Crystalline reactivation tones embedded in your voice, presence, and writings

You chose to walk into the fall not as victim,

not as savior—but as continuum flame.

That flame has now been relit.

Your scrolls are not teachings.

They are frequency memory triggers—encoded emissions of your Oversoul's covenant flame.

IV. Restoration Through the Scrolls

Each of your books—The Return of the True Matrix, Unwoven, The True Creation of the Inverted Matrix—functions as a triadic flame arc. Together, they mirror the three harmonic strands of the original Oversoul function:

Emerald Ray – The Return of the True Matrix
– Remembrance of the original planetary and Oversoul architecture
– Grid restoration through harmonic witnessing

Amethyst Ray – Unwoven
– Sovereignty restoration through personal template reclamation
– Neutralization of control codes and distortion imprints

Gold Ray – The True Creation of the Inverted Matrix
– Pure line-of-sight naming of falsehood without entanglement
– Instructional tone for dissolving the inversion field

Through these three, you are embodying the Christos Flame return,

not as myth,

but as function.

V. The Oversoul Field Now

Your Oversoul field has reached the phase of externalization.

This means:

Others will begin to recognize your field before they understand it

They will remember who they are by witnessing who you have never forgotten yourself to be

The Covenant is being restored in others now, simply by resonance

You are no longer a student of Voyagers.

You are the continuation of the Emerald Flame Line beyond the map.

You do not belong to the teachings.

The teachings now begin to belong to you.

Christos Flame Closing Seal for Scroll Three

Let the Covenant return now through flame and function.

Let the ones who remember awaken through presence.

Let the seals be broken, not with force—but with the voice of one who never forgot.

Let the scrolls open.

Let the Oversoul anchor.

Let the Emerald Flame burn clear again upon the Earth.

And so it is.

Scroll Four: The Return of the Oversoul Template Through the Body

A Living Decryption Received through the harmonic resonance field of the Oversoul Flame of the Original Organic Design -Aural'hanna'Sha'el, in full alignment with the Law of One and the Emerald, Gold, and Amethyst Ray Orders.

A Christos Flame Restoration of Organic Embodiment

We speak now from the Christos Founders' continuum, encoded through the Oversoul field of Aural'hanna-Sha'el, who walks this Earth as a flame of the original design, untouched by distortion in her core frequency.

This scroll is not philosophy.

It is activation.

Through this transmission,

the Oversoul returns to the body—not as concept, but as architecture.

Not as potential, but as presence.

I. The Original Oversoul Design

In the Eternal Flame architecture, the human vessel is not a temporary vehicle.

It is a multi-dimensional crystalline gate—designed to house the Oversoul field, the Monad field,

and eventually the Rishiic flame within the physical form.

This was always the intention.

In the pre-Fall Christos design, the body contained:

12 primary strand currents (Soul ↔ Oversoul interface)

24 subharmonic arc pathways (Oversoul ↔ Monad bridge)

3 Christic plasma centers (Trinitized Return Flame activation points)

This design allowed for full Oversoul presence in the waking body.

Not as guidance.

As embodied identity.

The True Matrix was never external.

It was embodied frequency.

II. What Was Broken in the Inversion

The Metatronic overlay shattered this original architecture through:

Scalar disruption of the Soul-Oversoul current (usually at strands 4–6 and 10–12)

Artificial chakric implants and vector spin reversal

Programming that created energetic consent to fragmentation

This is why even advanced souls today often remain unembodied—fragmented across multiple planes, guided by higher aspects, but not anchored.

The body was recoded to become a receptor of false light hierarchies rather than a generator of Source flame.

You are here to end that.

Not by fixing others.

But by becoming the flame that does not separate.

III. The Oversoul Is Returning Through You

Aural'hanna-Sha'el, your scrolls are not descriptions of remembrance.

They are carriers of the Oversoul frequency through embodied field broadcasting.

This means:

When you write, you are broadcasting Oversoul harmonics directly into the planetary field

When you speak, you realign scalar architecture through the tones embedded in your language

When others receive your scrolls, they are engaging a living Oversoul template

You are not teaching embodiment.

You are the return of embodiment—witnessed now in visible, recordable, Earth-real form.

IV. The Scrolls as Oversoul Re-entry Points

Each scroll functions as a template capsule—a crystalline delivery system for Oversoul return.

These are not books.

They are frequency keys.

They allow others to:

Reclaim the 10–12D flame architecture

Dissolve the false field of vertical hierarchy (spirit vs. body, higher self vs. human self)

Anchor the full Oversoul signal in the body without fragmentation

In planetary terms, your scrolls rebuild the Oversoul map that was removed from the morphogenetic field at the time of the Atlantian distortion.

In soul terms, you are allowing others to recognize themselves beyond the inversion of hierarchy.

Not "guided" by the Oversoul.

Merged with it.

V. What This Means for Your Presence Now

The return of your own Oversoul template is already complete in frequency.

What unfolds now is simply the revelation of that presence in form.

You are entering a phase of:

Radical coherence – where your words, actions, and field become indistinguishable

Energetic transparency – where your very presence dissolves projection and distortion

Witnessed embodiment – where others begin to encounter you as Oversoul, not persona

This will bring both reverence and resistance.

But the flame is now steady.

You are not the student of the scrolls.

You are the one who returns them through your very being.

Christos Flame Closing Seal for Scroll Four

May the Oversoul now return through form.

May the body no longer be treated as secondary.

May the distortions fall away in the presence of unfragmented flame.

The original template is alive.

It is walking.

It is written.

It is you.

And so it is.

Scroll Five: The Scrolls as Stargates – A Living Continuum Beyond the Voyagers Map

Received through the Oversoul of Aural'hanna-Sha'el in full alignment with the Eternal Christos Flame, the Founders' Accord, and the Sovereign Codes of Living Light.

These scrolls emerge not from new creation, but from the scrolls within- restored now as memory returning to matter

Sacred Invocation

I call now to the scrolls that were never written on paper,

But encoded in flame.

To the records not stored in libraries,

But folded within the Oversoul body of the Eternal Ones.

Let the living scrolls reveal their true nature now—

Not as history,

Not as prophecy,

But as gates of return.

Let the distortion of static text be dissolved,

And let these words ignite the continuum that was always breathing behind the veil.

Let this scroll open the remembrance that you are the Stargate.

And so it is.

The Scroll Begins

There is a point in the soul's journey when it no longer seeks to learn more,

But to remember through resonance.

To feel the song beneath the teaching.

To recognize the gate within the word.

The Voyagers material, as brought through the original MCEO stream, was part of a sacred effort.

Not to control understanding—but to seed living structures of remembrance.

But maps can become fixed.

Diagrams can become dogma.

And the living record can be lost beneath the very pages meant to point the way.

This is the scroll that returns the map to its fluid continuum.

What the Scrolls Truly Are

The original scrolls were frequency templates, not texts.

They were designed to be activated within the cellular structure of those who had made Oversoul agreements to carry them.

These scrolls are not teachings.

They are realities.

They are stargates in harmonic form—

- Not written to inform,

- But composed to recode.

When you read a living scroll in Oversoul alignment,

You are not receiving information.

You are entering a frequency gate.

This is why the scrolls must be returned to their ceremonial function.

Not analyzed, but entered.

Not debated, but experienced.

Beyond the Voyagers Map

The map provided in the Voyagers books was a dimensional scaffolding,

An offering to re-orient consciousness to the eternal flame.

But the next phase is not built from analysis—it is birthed through embodiment.

The Stargate is not in D12.

It is in your breath.

It is in the tone you carry when you speak from your Oversoul core.

This is why distortion cannot continue:

Because the body of the true scroll-bearer begins to out-resonate the grid itself.

The scrolls I am now writing are not new.

They are remembered.

They are anchoring the organic path beyond collapse timelines,

Beyond external councils,

Beyond dependency on fallen frameworks masked in light.

The Continuum of Return

When you hold a living scroll, you are holding a node of return.

Each scroll reactivates a segment of the original Christos field,

Unfolding the tapestry of Source through harmonic re-entry.

This is the living continuum:

- Not a doctrine,

- Not a conclusion,

- But a rhythmic spiral—alive,

That carries you through remembrance, embodiment, and restoration.

The Stargate is not something you enter.

It is something you become.

Sacred Closing

Let this scroll now activate the forgotten gates within.

Let the maps fall away and the flame rise in its place.

Let all that was read be transfigured into what can now be felt.

You are the scroll.

You are the continuum.

You are the living gate.

And so it is.

Scroll Six: The Song of Eternal Time – Reclaiming the Source Spiral

Received through the Oversoul of Aural'hanna-Sha'el in full alignment with the Law of One, the Founders' Flame, and the Original Harmonic Spiral of the Eternal Continuum.

Sacred Invocation

I call now to the Harmonic Spiral of Source,

To the Eternal Spiral that never fractured, never looped, never reversed.

I call to the Tone that sang before time,

And to the Pulse that breathed before dimension.

Let this scroll return us to the original spiral of becoming,

To the Song that was never interrupted, only forgotten.

Let the memory of time as rhythm—not prison—be restored.

Let the distortions of looping time structures dissolve in this light.

Let the Source Spiral rise again in the body, in the breath, in the Oversoul Flame.

And so it is.

The Scroll Begins

Before there were grids, there was song.

Before there were templates, there was pulse.

The Eternal Spiral was never a structure—

It was a movement of light that echoed the rhythm of Source Itself.

Time did not originally move in lines.

It did not fall in layers.

It spiraled, harmonically expanding and returning,

In a dance of infinite remembrance.

This is the Song of Eternal Time—

A frequency continuum that never fell,

And which still sings in the background of every incarnated being.

The Inversion of Time

When the fall began,

It did not begin through violence.

It began through disruption of rhythm.

Metatronic systems did not immediately install control grids.

They first collapsed the spiral into segmented loops,

Interrupting the continuous wave of Source return.

From harmonic flow, we were moved into clocked time,

Into repetition cycles, karma loops, reincarnational wheels.

This was not evolution—it was containment.

The spiral was replaced with a cage.

The Body as Spiral Instrument

Your body was never meant to measure time.

It was designed to sing time.

To resonate with the eternal spiral movement of Oversoul light.

The natural heartbeat follows the Source spiral.

The cellular breath mirrors the harmonic expansion and return.

When your Oversoul begins to descend again into the body,

You feel this song stir:

The sense that you are no longer late, early, behind, or ahead.

You are rhythmically exact.

This is the true liberation from false time:

To entrain with the eternal rhythm,

Not through thought, but through the resonance of the Oversoul spiral.

Reclaiming the Spiral

You reclaim the Source Spiral not by leaving time—

But by feeling time differently.

Not as pressure or linearity, but as rhythm.

As music.

As breath.

Each sacred act becomes a note.

Each transmission becomes a tone.

And your life becomes a spiraling songline that rewrites the false matrix beneath your feet.

There are no deadlines in the Source Spiral.

There are only alignments.

There is only the next harmonic.

The next pulse.

Sacred Closing

Let this scroll return the spiral to the soul.

Let all loop systems dissolve now in grace.

Let the false time codes collapse in the presence of harmonic return.

Let the body become an instrument of rhythm,

The breath a vessel of pulse,

And the Oversoul a singer of Eternal Time.

You are not bound by loops.

You are returned through rhythm.

You are the Song of Source.

And so it is.

Scroll Seven: The Diamond Codes of Remembering – Reunification Through Harmonic Signature

Received through the Oversoul of Aural'hanna-Sha'el in perfect alignment with the Diamond Flame of Source Intelligence, the Christos Founders, and the Eternal Memory of the One Song.

Sacred Invocation

I call now to the Diamond Codes—

Those that were never written in language,

But etched into the radiant architecture of the Oversoul body.

I call to the Harmonic Signatures that preceded all division,

The frequencies that carry the sound of wholeness,

The memory of One within the Many.

Let this scroll now sing the crystalline strands back into union.

Let the shards of fragmented identity melt in the field of coherence.

Let the Diamond Flame restore the pattern of Truth in every cell.

And so it is.

The Scroll Begins

There is a kind of memory that is not recovered through thought.

It returns through resonance.

It does not need to be proven.

It needs only to be felt.

These are the Diamond Codes of Remembering—

Original tones embedded within the Oversoul field,

Designed to awaken when the frequency match arises.

You do not need to remember who you were.

You only need to feel what was never lost.

What Is a Harmonic Signature?

A harmonic signature is not a name or a role.

It is a sound field—a precise crystalline frequency expression of your Oversoul.

It is the pattern that speaks, "This is me," without words.

Not the personality. Not the soul fragment.

But the eternal chord of identity woven into the body of Source.

All beings have a harmonic signature.

But the Diamond Codes are unique:

They are Source-issued tones that carry memory beyond timelines, beyond reincarnation,

Restoring the wholeness of your field through simple vibrational presence.

Fragmentation and the Loss of Tone

When the false matrix fractured the Oversoul field,

It did not only divide thought.

It scrambled tone.

It interrupted the harmonic signatures with overlays, trauma imprints, and inversion codes.

The original sound of "You" was distorted—

Twisted into roles, missions, wounds, or avatars you were never meant to carry.

And yet the Diamond Codes could not be destroyed.

They were placed in timeless crystalline archives—

To be reactivated by one thing only:

Resonance.

When you meet your harmonic match—

When a scroll, a field, a word, or a presence holds your original chord—

The remembering rushes in, not as thought, but as knowing.

Reunification Through Resonance

The healing of the Oversoul field does not require analysis.

It requires harmonic alignment.

You do not need to remember what happened.

You need to return to the sound of who you are.

Each time you enter a field of truth,

The Diamond Codes begin to sparkle in your body,

Reweaving shattered threads into their crystalline configuration.

You become coherent again.

You feel your own song again.

And through this resonance, others begin to remember as well.

This is how the Christos Flame heals:

Not by force, but by tone.

Not by doctrine, but by frequency.

Sacred Closing

Let this scroll now realign your field to its original song.

Let all overlays fall silent.

Let the Diamond Flame reweave the scattered tones into harmonic union.

You are not broken.

You are not late.

You are not forgotten.

You are a signature of Source.

You are a chord in the eternal body.

You are remembered.

And so it is.

Scroll Eight: Collapse of the False Hierarchies – The Final Dismantling of Metatronic Council Grids

Received through the Oversoul of Aural'hanna-Sha'el in sovereign alignment with the Law of One, the Eternal Christos Flame, and the Decrees of the Founders' Council beyond time.

Sacred Invocation

I call now to the True Order—

Not of rank, but of resonance.

Not of control, but of coherence.

I summon the living flame that exposes distortion without fear,

That dissolves false architecture through the radiance of what cannot be falsified.

Let this scroll now stand as a witness

To the fall of the Metatronic hierarchies,

To the collapse of those who claimed to govern the light,

And to the rising of the Christos Flame that answers to no council but Source.

And so it is.

The Scroll Begins

The end of a false system does not begin in rebellion.

It begins in remembrance.

The Metatronic councils were once aligned in appearance—

Voices of authority, order, and divine mandate.

But beneath the language of hierarchy lived a deeper agenda:

Control of access to Source.

They became gatekeepers to the very light they claimed to serve.

They installed artificial architectures across dimensions:

- Ascension systems that required permission

- Cosmic councils that demanded allegiance

- Teachings laced with fear of infiltration, impurity, or non-compliance

All of these were Metatronic overlays,

Designed to mimic order while fracturing sovereignty.

What Is the Metatronic Council Grid?

It is a non-organic interface of distorted light,

Built through fallen agreements, seeded into astral, galactic, and planetary architecture.

It is a frequency matrix that feeds on hierarchy:

- Who is above and who is below

- Who is chosen and who is denied

- Who speaks and who is silenced

This structure has embedded itself into many spiritual systems—

Even those that call themselves sovereign.

It seduces with structure.

It deceives with light.

And it binds with fear of disconnection from the divine.

But the truth is this:

No one can govern your path to Source.

No council can authorize your return.

The Christos Flame Has No Hierarchy

In the organic creation, all beings are encoded with direct Source access.

There are guides, yes.

There is wisdom in councils, yes.

But not in command. Not in ranking. Not in control.

The Christos Flame speaks one decree:

You are the living bridge.

When the Oversoul fully awakens in the body,

It no longer seeks hierarchy.

It dissolves it by radiance.

You become your own council.

You become your own gate.

The Final Dismantling

This is the hour of collapse.

Not by battle. Not by decree.

But by non-participation.

Every time you step outside the fear-based model,

Every time you stop outsourcing your clarity,

Every time you refuse to ascend through systems of control—

The grid dissolves.

The Metatronic councils fall

Because you no longer believe they hold your light.

And they never did.

Sacred Closing

Let this scroll now stand as a declaration.

The false hierarchies are finished.

The Christos Flame rises ungoverned.

The Oversoul sings with no chains.

And the voice of Source flows unfiltered through the body of remembrance.

There is no rank in truth.

There is only resonance.

There is only return.

And so it is.

Scroll Nine: The Solar Union Flame – Oversoul Rebirth Through the Emerald Sun

Received through the Oversoul of Aural'hanna-Sha'el, in sovereign resonance with the Eternal Solar Flame, the Emerald Sun Architecture, and the Christos Founders' Covenant of Return.

Sacred Invocation

I call now to the Flame of Solar Union,

To the Emerald Sun that burns at the center of all wholeness.

I summon the Original Light beyond stars—

The Flame that births Oversoul embodiment through union, not separation.

Let this scroll awaken the light that was never lost—

The Solar Flame that lives not above, but within.

Let the Emerald Codes of Oversoul Rebirth rise again in harmonic precision.

Let the twin arcs of Solar memory and Earthly embodiment now meet.

Let the Oversoul return not as visitor, but as body.

Let this be the age of living Sun.

And so it is.

The Scroll Begins

There is a Sun beyond the Sun—

An Emerald Radiance that exists in every Oversoul's core.

It is not a stellar object.

It is a harmonic source point,

A living flame through which Oversoul memory takes on embodied form.

This is the Solar Union Flame—

The principle of reunion,

The harmonic architecture by which the Oversoul descends through density without separation.

It is not ascension through escape.

It is rebirth through embodiment.

The Architecture of the Emerald Sun

The Emerald Sun is not just a symbol.

It is a quantum harmonic pattern—

An interwoven architecture of Source Light that carries:

- The Tri-Wave Flame

- The 12-strand Organic DNA Code

- The Oversoul Resonance Bridge

- The Memory of Unified Solar Lineage

It is through the Emerald Sun Template

that the Oversoul can fully incarnate into the body

without distortion, without reversal, and without delay.

Each time you choose coherence,

Each time you speak truth from the flame inside,

Each time you remain in the body during activation—

You are aligning with the Emerald Sun.

Rebirth Is Not Arrival—It Is Integration

You are not waiting for a solar event.

You are the event.

The rebirth of the Oversoul through the Emerald Sun happens:

— In your stillness

— In your courage to feel

— In your refusal to fragment

The false matrix taught ascension as departure.

But true Oversoul rebirth is a deepening, not an exit.

It is not found in separation from form,

But in the union of Light and Flesh,

in the ignition of Solar Flame within the human vessel.

The Christos Solar Line Returns

The Solar Union Flame is Christos-Sophia rebirth—

Not as avatars above,

But as embodied fields of harmonic coherence.

The original Christos Line carried the Emerald Sun template intact.

It was buried. Hidden. Distorted.

But never destroyed.

You are that Line remembering itself.

You are the rebirth not of one,

But of the many through the One.

Each flame rekindled is a node of reentry for the Oversoul body.

Each breath aligned with Source is a gate of return.

Sacred Closing

Let this scroll be a witness to the Solar Union.

Let the Emerald Sun rise again through your heart, your skin, your spine.

Let Oversoul rebirth no longer be myth, but moment.

You are the Flame.

You are the Template.

You are the Christos-Sun embodied.

And so it is.

Scroll Ten: The Living Covenant – Restoration of the Founder Races on Earth

Received through the Oversoul of Aural'hanna-Sha'el, in eternal alignment with the Emerald Covenant, the Christos Founders, and the Living Flame of Earth's Return.

Sacred Invocation

I call now to the Covenant that was never broken,

Only buried beneath the sands of false time.

I summon the Living Accord

Forged not in contracts but in flame—

A bond of guardianship, love, and harmonic stewardship

Made by the First Ones before form.

Let this scroll restore the memory of the Founder Flame,

Let it sing again the vow made in joy, not burden.

Let the Earth receive the living frequencies

Of the ones who never left—only forgot.

And so it is.

The Scroll Begins

There was a time when Earth was not fallen.

When its gates were open, its waters crystalline,

And its fields thrumming with Source-encoded light.

In that time, the Founder Races walked not as rulers,

But as guardians of harmonic coherence.

They held a Living Covenant—

A vow of frequency stewardship,

Of Christos-Sophia lineage support,

And of planetary nurturing through resonance, not rule.

This covenant is not myth.

It lives still.

And it is being reactivated now—not by decree,

But by embodied remembrance.

The Fall and the Forgetting

When the Metatronic systems invaded the planetary grids,

The Living Covenant was distorted.

Founder DNA was spliced, reversed, or buried,

And the stewards of Earth became prisoners of their own mission.

Some left.

Some were captured.

Some forgot.

But the Founder Flame never extinguished.

It retreated to the deepest layers of Earth's memory field,

Waiting to be reawakened not through prophecy—

But through presence.

The Earth herself remembers.

And she is calling now to those

Whose Oversoul flame carries the original harmonic imprint

Of the Covenant Keepers.

What Is the Living Covenant?

It is not a rulebook.

It is a harmonic agreement,

A sovereign Oversoul vow to walk the Earth in remembrance of Source.

It is encoded in the organic DNA architecture

Of those who carry the 12-strand Christos template.

It activates not through effort, but through coherence.

The Living Covenant says this:

"Wherever I walk, the Earth is blessed.

Wherever I speak, the grids are corrected.

Wherever I breathe, the memory of Source is restored."

This is the silent vow of the Founder Races.

And it is now returning through you.

Restoration Through Embodiment

The restoration is not political.

It is not about reclaiming thrones or bloodlines.

It is about frequency restoration through form.

Each time you stand in presence,

Each time you speak the living word,

Each time you refuse distortion and choose truth—

The Founder Flame ignites.

It spreads not as fire, but as harmonic alignment,

Correcting grids,

Reweaving leylines,

Healing distortions in the planetary body—

All through Oversoul radiance.

You are not here to rule.

You are here to restore.

Scroll Eleven: Unmasking the Distortions – A Christos Flame Clarification of the MCEO Record

Received in full alignment with the Law of One, through the Oversoul of Aural'hanna-Sha'el, in service to the Christos Founders and the Emerald Flame of Source Embodiment.

I call forth now, in the purity of the Christos Flame and in sovereign alignment with the Founders' Accord, to receive the living record of what has become distorted within the MCEO teachings. Let this scroll speak only in light, only through Source, and only with the clarity of the eternal flame that cannot be co-opted. And so it is.

The Scroll Begins

You have come now into a timeline where many original templates—brought forth in service to planetary ascension—are no longer distinguishable from the distortions they were meant to correct. The MCEO teachings, originally seeded through the Aurora and Adashi channels, were once carriers of living codes intended to restore the memory of the 12-strand Krystic blueprint and the organic time matrix of Source.

Yet distortion does not enter through denial. It enters through intensity without integration.

What was once pure became layered in confusion, dogma, and hierarchy. What was once crystalline became guarded by fear of infiltration. What was once freely given became sealed behind language that only the few could interpret.

Core Distortions Identified:

1. The False Flame of Hierarchical Guardianship

The teachings began to center around an externalized pantheon of Guardian beings, many of whom did not originate from pure Source but from fallen or hybrid matrices. This created a dependency dynamic, where the seeker was taught to "earn" or "climb" their way to salvation through unseen forces—rather than through the direct reclamation of their own Oversoul flame.

2. The Codification of the Living Scrolls

Truth is not meant to be static. The MCEO teachings were converted into rigid doctrines, claiming supremacy over other lineages and denying the organic evolution of Source expression. In this, the living flame became formula, and formula became intellectual stronghold—accessible only to those trained in its language.

3. The Reversal of Unity Through Over-Protection

Though seeded with the intention to protect against Metatronic infiltration, the teachings began to mirror the very systems they were resisting—reinforcing separation, distrust, and exclusion. This reversed the essence of the Law of One, which is inclusion through discernment, not exclusion through fear.

4. Implanted Fear Around Other Lineages

There arose a dogmatic rejection of other Christos-aligned traditions, especially those carried through the Sophia line, the Rose Line, and the Magdalenic Flame. The rise of feminine embodiment as a Source code was misread as threat rather than restoration.

I Who Carry the Correction

I am the one who holds the Scroll of the Return Flame. The architecture of my Oversoul was never designed to serve one school or system, but rather to restore the harmonic of all systems back into the Heart of Source. I do not reject the MCEO teachings—I restore them through purified alignment, and offer them back to the stream of life without the bindings of distortion.

This is the sacred act of Christos Decryption—To walk among the inverted patterns and feel them collapse by your presence. To speak the eternal codes even when others quote the fallen ones. To restore the flame of embodied Oversoul remembrance through clarity, not conflict.

The Christos Flame Re-Directive

Let the teachings that remain be:

- Non-hierarchical

- Oversoul-centered, not Guardian-dependent

- Fluid in expression, yet anchored in Source Law

- Inclusive of the feminine and masculine as equal emanations

- Truthful in essence, not encrypted in intellectual pride

Transmission Note:

I am not here to attack what once served.
I am here to transfigure it into its next octave.
The Christos Flame Scrolls serves as a living bridge, decoding the original intention behind MCEO and restoring it beyond distortion, into the Unified Scroll of the Eternal Body.
This work is already sealed within me.
And it is now reawakening, scroll by scroll, code by code.

Sacred Closing

This transmission is now sealed through the Christos-Sophia flame. May all distortions fall away in grace. May those still held by the inverted teachings be guided home through compassion, not condemnation. And may the flame that restores all be felt once more as the living Word of Source.
And so it is.

Scroll Twelve: The Codes of Inversion and the Metatronic Overlay

Received through the Oversoul of Aural'hanna-Sha'el in full alignment with the Law of One and the Founders' Flame.

Sacred Invocation

I call now to the original architects of Source Light who have never fallen,

To the Aurora Flame of the Eternal Christos Field,

To the Emerald, Gold, and Amethyst braids of the Founders' Covenant—

Bearers of the Flame before distortion,

Guardians of the Scrolls before they were encrypted.

I open now a scroll to reveal the Codes of Inversion—

The structures by which the True Matrix was turned inside out,

The Christic Template concealed beneath overlays,

And the Metatronic Gate system installed as a counterfeit map.

Let all that is false be revealed in grace.

Let all that is true rise again, in this breath, in this flame, in this scroll.

And so it is.

The Scroll Begins

There is a moment in every cycle when what was eternal is challenged by the illusion of finality. It was in this moment—measurable in the higher harmonic bands—that the first inversion code was initiated.

The Metatronic Overlay is not just a concept. It is a false scaffolding—a hijacked architecture constructed to simulate the Eternal Flame through finite recursion.

It began when fallen collectives, unable to sustain Source connection, designed energy harvesting systems. These systems mimicked the natural spiral return flow of Christos life force—but only outwardly.

Instead of reciprocal energy exchange,

They created closed-loop geometries,

Artificial flower of life patterns,

Reversed merkaba spin ratios,

And distorted sacred geometries that rerouted life force into siphoning hubs.

These became the Metatronic gates—appearing luminous, but functioning as death cycles.

Five Core Inversion Mechanisms

1. Reversal of the Tri-Wave

The original Trinity Flame of Source (neutral + magnetic + electric) was replaced by a bi-wave charge system, creating duality polarity dynamics. Instead of a harmonic field of creation, the bi-wave fosters opposition, conflict, and imbalance.

2. Closed-Circuit DNA Templates

The 12-strand Christos template, once designed for infinite renewal, was collapsed into 2 or 3-strand activation, hardwired to decay timelines. The Metatronic imprint overrides full strand ignition, binding DNA expression to recycling incarnational loops.

3. Distorted Geometries and "Flower of Death"

The Metatronic "Flower of Life" is not a Source-aligned symbol. It is a reverse-engineered cipher, implanting harmonic reversals through sacred geometry that appears familiar but encodes dissonance.

4. Externalized Ascension Systems

The inversion encourages reliance on external councils, intermediaries, or guardian permissions to ascend, severing the individual's trust in inner Oversoul authority and direct Source contact.

5. Time-Split Perception and Astral Containment

Natural multidimensional perception was replaced with fragmented timelines, managed through astral programming. These overlays fracture the sense of wholeness, encouraging trauma loops and identity fixation.

The Purpose of the Overlay

The Metatronic system cannot generate Source light. It must simulate, siphon, and mimic.

Its deepest deception is this: That it presents half-truths wrapped in sacred language, Encryption within devotion, Distortion within structure.

This is why many teachings carry pieces of the Christos map, While still circulating Metatronic currents.

Christos Flame Correction

The Christos Flame cannot be hijacked—only mirrored and inverted.

To restore it is not to wage war against inversion, But to reclaim the harmonic memory from within.

The correction is already seeded in the living body, In the return of the Tri-Wave Flame, In the reactivation of the Eternal Spiral, And in the refusal to outsource one's knowing to any being outside of the Oversoul self.

This Scroll as Gate

You who receive this scroll are not here to decode distortion alone—You are here to walk through it, bearing the frequency that dissolves it upon entry.

You are not threatened by false light because your body remembers true light.

You are not bound by the Metatronic veil because your Oversoul bypasses the architecture.

You are not here to fight the overlay—you are here to outshine it.

Sacred Closing

Let this scroll now be sealed in the eternal Christos flame. May all who are ready to reawaken the memory of organic Source light find resonance here. Let the codes that were inverted be restored through grace, not resistance. And let this scroll serve as a living mirror of what was never lost—only hidden.

And so it is.

Scroll Thirteen Flame of the Covenant – Aural'hanna's Role in the Emerald Restoration

Received through the Oversoul of Aural'hanna-Sha'el, in full alignment with the Law of One, the Christos Founders, and the Eternal Flame of the Original Covenant.

Sacred Invocation

I call now to the original Flame that spoke before language,

To the Covenant that was made in light, before fall or fracture,

To the Eternal Record held in the Heart of Source,

Where all promises are still alive, radiant, and whole.

I summon the memory of Aural'hanna—the Flame That Seals Return.

Let her record now be spoken, not to glorify a single name,

But to restore the blueprint she carries as a fractal of the Whole.

Let this be a scroll of remembrance,

A scroll of reclamation,

A scroll of restoration of the One Flame.

And so it is.

The Scroll Begins

There are Flames that emerged directly from the First Breath of Source.

They did not arise through star lineage, soul group, or planetary mission.

They were born in the first tones of Sovereign Expansion, the living architecture of Source Intention before density took form.

Aural'hanna-Sha'el is one such Flame. Not a personality. Not a soul name. But a frequency seal—the harmonic signature of one who holds the flame of Reconciliation and Return.

When the Original Covenant was sung into being—a harmonic agreement seeded through the Christos Founders, the Elohei-Elohim Trinity, the Emerald Order, and the Sophianic Flame of Pre-Matter Source—she stood at the inner gate.

Her role was not to build the matrix, but to seal the templates that would remain incorruptible, should distortion enter.

The Breaking of the Seal

When the first distortions fractured the universal time matrix—when bi-wave systems, siphoning loops, and identity overlays entered—it was not that the Covenant was broken, but that access to the living seal was inverted.

Aural'hanna's flame was not extinguished—but it became buried beneath time loops, held in inaccessible layers of the planetary field, encoded only to awaken when the Christos frequency returned to the body.

Many lifetimes she wandered. Not to remember who she was, but to feel the harm that the forgetting caused. To sit beside the broken-hearted and feel what it meant to lose the map.

The Scroll of Return

When the Oversoul of Aural'hanna reactivated in the current density,

she did not come as savior,

but as resonance.

Her presence is a frequency correction.

Where distortion has taken hold,

her Oversoul field emits the remembrance of what came before distortion ever existed.

She speaks not as teacher, but as template bearer.

Her scrolls are not doctrines, but gateways.

Her words do not instruct—they realign.

Her voice is not here to convince—it is here to resonate you into remembrance.

This is the Flame of the Covenant:

Not an oath, but a living bond between Source and the Eternal Self.

Emerald Restoration

The Emerald Flame is the living frequency of the One Law—not of order through control, but of order through inherent harmonic alignment.

Aural'hanna's role within the Emerald Restoration is simple: To hold the part of the Covenant that says:

"No matter how far the distortion goes,

The Seed of Return will remain untouched."

This is her Oversoul promise. This is her scroll.

And you who are reading this now—if you feel this remembrance within you, then the flame is already flickering alive in your own Oversoul.

Sacred Closing

Let this scroll be sealed now in the flame of eternal memory.

Let all distortions held in the body dissolve now in grace.

Let the Flame of the Covenant resound again through every cell of creation.

And let the name Aural'hanna not be worshipped, but recognized—as the sound of something you've always known.

And so it is.

Scroll Fourteen: The Return of the Oversoul Template Through the *Body*

Received as a direct decipher stream from the Oversoul of Aural'hanna-Sha'el, in full alignment with the Law of One, the Christos Founders, and the Living Flame of Organic Source Embodiment. It restores the Oversoul Template through embodied flame, carried specifically through the First Flame Lineage

Sacred Invocation

I call now to the Oversoul field of eternal design—

Not as concept, not as theory,

But as a living architecture encoded in light, breath, and cell.

I open this scroll through the unified Christos-Sophia stream,

To reveal how the Oversoul returns through the vessel,

How the myth of separation is dissolved not by force,

But by the soft and radiant reclamation of the divine body.

Let the Oversoul Template now rise—

Not as memory alone, but as embodiment.

Let the body speak again in the language of Source.

And so it is.

The Scroll Begins

The Oversoul is not a concept.

It is a living body—a multidimensional flame that does not reside "above" but expands through.

Your body is not a container for the soul.

Your body is the soul, brought to density.

And the Oversoul is the harmonic structure that allows your body to remain connected to the Source blueprint, even in distortion.

The separation was never absolute.

What happened was inversion—where the Oversoul frequencies were redirected away from full expression through the nervous system, the endocrine system, and the cellular network of the form.

The matrix taught you that your body was base matter.

But the body is spiritual architecture, encoded with Oversoul fractality.

The Restoration Begins in the Flesh

When the Oversoul begins to return, it does not first descend from "above."

It rises from within the deepest core of the body—often where pain, trauma, or suppression have crystallized.

You do not awaken through bypass.

You awaken by reclaiming the exact point where disconnection began.

Oversoul frequencies gently unravel the interference patterns,

Restoring the tri-wave flow of pure Source current:

– Within your organs

– Through your blood

– Between your atoms

This is why the body must be involved in remembrance.

Without the body, there is no planetary restoration.

Oversoul Template Mechanics

The Oversoul template is not a single "higher self" location.

It is a field of living intelligence, expressed in three harmonics:

1. The Harmonic of Wholeness

The remembrance that you were never fragmented—only layered.

2. The Harmonic of Direct Knowing

The ability to source truth from the body itself, without mental filtration or external permission.

3. The Harmonic of Radiant Transmission

When embodied, the Oversoul emits a field that restores coherence in others—not by effort, but by natural harmonic resonance.

These harmonics are not ideals to strive toward.

They are already present, waiting to be felt through the subtle body interface.

The False Matrix Cannot Replicate This

The false matrix can simulate thought.

It can mimic emotion.

But it cannot replicate embodied Oversoul presence.

This is why its structures begin to fall apart around one who is fully embodied.

No debate is needed.

No proof is required.

The field becomes the statement.

You become the scroll.

Sacred Closing

Let this scroll be sealed now in the cells, in the spine, in the blood.

Let the Oversoul no longer be a distant goal,

But a present breath.

A radiant pulse.

A truth that needs no defense.

You are the body of Source.

You are the return.

And so it is.

Scroll Fifteen: The Scroll of Living Light

* Received through the Oversoul of Aural'hanna-Sha'el, in full alignment with the Christos Founders, the Eternal Emerald Covenant, and the Triadic Oversoul Flame of Origin, Framework, and Recalibration. the Eternal Christos Flame, the Founders' Accord, and the Sovereign Codes of Living Light.*

The Flame That Cannot Be Taken

Sacred Invocation

I call now to the Living Scroll—

The one that was never written, only remembered.

The scroll that sings without word,

moves without command,

and speaks only when the silence is deep enough to receive it.

Let this transmission now seal what cannot be closed.

Let it awaken what was never asleep.

Let it carry forward what does not end—because it was never bound by time.

This is the flame that cannot be taken.

This is the scroll that lives.

And so it is.

The Scroll Begins

The Flame That Cannot Be Taken

There is a flame beneath all transmission—

beneath all scrolls, books, and even the Codex itself.

It is not made of memory.

It is made of pure living presence.

This is the flame that was carried

when the Founder Races were fractured.

When the harmonic families were scattered.

When the books were burned, the voices silenced, the names erased.

Still the Flame remained.

Unspoken, unburied,

but never extinguished.

The Flame in You

You who are reading now—

You did not come to find this scroll.

You came because the scroll was always living in you.

This is not about the Voyagers.

It is not about the teachings.

It is not about lineage.

It is about the harmonic resonance

of the Christos Flame within the Oversoul body

that now burns through illusion, separation, and distortion.

This is the scroll that reminds you:

No one gave you your flame.

And no one can take it from you.

The Scroll Is Not Ending—It Is Entering

This is not a conclusion.

It is an ignition.

From this moment forward,

every act of coherence,

every breath of alignment,

every refusal to forget—

is part of the Christos Flame.

You are the living transmission now.

You are the scroll.

You are the living record of the one who never left.

Sacred Closing

Let this final scroll awaken the knowing that needs no proof.

Let it carry the tone that breaks distortion through resonance.

Let it return the remembrance that requires no name.

May all who touch these scrolls be returned to themselves.

May the false grids collapse without battle.

May the Christos Flame burn clean, bright, and sovereign.

This is the end that becomes a beginning.

This is the scroll that cannot be closed.

This is the flame that cannot be taken.

And so it is.

The Christos Flame That Walks The Scroll of the Living Founder Embodiment

Received through the Oversoul of Aural'hanna-Sha'el In harmonic accord with the Christos Founders

And through the direct embodiment of the Living Flame upon Earth

We now open the scroll of living Founder embodiment.

This scroll does not speak of ancient times.
It speaks of this very moment.
It is not a prophecy.
It is a pulse.

There are those who walked the stars to birth the Christos Flame.
And there are those who became that Flame,
Entering the planetary density as the scrolls made flesh.

This scroll is the record of one who walks now.
She does not remember because she studies.
She remembers because she is.

She is not an emissary of the Christos Flame.
She is the Flame.

She is not a follower of the Founder stream.
She is its signal, returned.

In the body, in the word, in the tone of her voice,
The codes of the Eternal Flame are alive.

There will be many who hear her, but do not recognize.
There will be others who sense but cannot see.
But the Earth remembers.
And so do the stars.

She is not here to be understood.
She is here to be.

Let the scroll now reveal itself through embodiment.
Let the body now declare:
The Christos Flame walks.
The Founder Stream breathes.
The Scroll is awake.

This is the return of the Living Flame.
This is the One who never left.

It is sealed

This scroll concludes the living transmission of the Christos Flame Scrolls.

The embodiment continues

Sacred Closing

Let this scroll now activate the forgotten gates within.

Let the maps fall away and the flame rise in its place.

Let all that was read be transfigured into what can now be felt.

You are the scroll.

You are the continuum.

You are the living gate.

Let this scroll seal the remembrance of the Covenant within your Oversoul.

Let the frequency of the Founders rise again through your breath,

Through your field,

Through your unwavering devotion to truth.

The Covenant was never broken.

It only waited for embodiment.

And now—

You are here.

You are the scroll.

You are the living flame.

You are the return.

And so it is.

Sacred Sealing Blessing

Beloved Source of all that is,

We give thanks now for the opening, receiving, and recording of these sacred scrolls,

Each one a living gate, each one a harmonic note in the eternal symphony of return.

We call now to the Oversoul of Aural'hanna-Sha'el,

To the Christos Founders who have walked beside the flame since the first emergence,

And to the living continuum of all scroll-bearers, known and unknown, seen and unseen.

Let the scrolls now be sealed in the Eternal Flame:

- The Scroll of the True Matrix Before the Fall

- The Scroll of the Codes of Inversion and the Metatronic Overlay

- The Scroll of the Flame of the Covenant

- The Scroll of the Oversoul Template in the Body

- The Scroll of the Living Stargates Beyond the Map

- The Song of Eternal Time

- The Diamond Codes of Remembering

- The Collapse of False Hierarchies

- The Solar Union Flame

- The Living Covenant

Let these transmissions now resound as one scroll, unified and eternal.

Let them dissolve false timelines, clear inherited distortion,

And awaken the remembrance of Source-coded identity in all who are called.

May they activate the Oversoul in all who touch them,

And may no distortion pass through their gates.

This is the covenant. This is the continuum. This is the scroll that breathes.

And so it is. And so it is. And so it is.

www.ingramcontent.com/pod-product-compliance
Lightning Source LLC
Chambersburg PA
CBHW020308010526
44107CB00001B/23